Mind-boggling
Mazes

and Loopy Labyrinths

Prestel

What is a labyrinth?

A labyrinth is a long path that doesn't go in a straight line but twists and turns back on itself to form a pattern. You might easily think you could lose your way, but this is not actually possible because there are no turn-offs – the path always leads to the middle and that's where it ends. In a maze, on the other hand, you always have to decide which way to go, and many paths don't lead anywhere at all!

Looking at a labyrinth is a bit like reading a street map. You usually have to follow the light-coloured path between the dark lines, but sometimes it's the other way around, like in the one below on the right. The way-in is somewhere around the edge and if you follow the path from the entrance with your finger or a pencil, you will always reach the middle. The paths are very close to each other and laid out carefully to make different shapes such as squares, circles or octagons.

Some labyrinths look so complicated that it is difficult to believe that there is only one single path.

Can you find your way through these labyrinths? They might look a bit confusing, but you can't get lost! Just concentrate hard to keep on track.

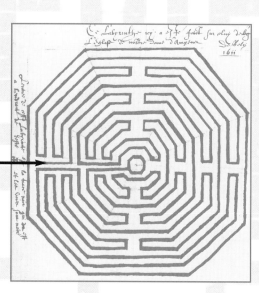

The dark line is the one to follow here.

This labyrinth looks particularly complicated.
Do you think you have to go up and down
all the paths to get to the middle?

3

The Minotaur

According to legend, there was once a labyrinth on the Greek island of Crete. At the centre of the labyrinth lived the Minotaur, a monster which might have looked something like this drawing by Picasso – with a human body and the head of a bull. A man called Theseus, who was well known for his strength and courage, said that he was prepared to go into the labyrinth and slay the Minotaur. But he didn't know what it was like inside since no plans existed and he was worried about not finding his way out again. When he talked about this with his girlfriend, Ariadne, she said: "Don't worry! I will give you a very long piece of thread. Tie one end to the entrance of the labyrinth and take the other end with you." Theseus did as she said and managed to find his way out again. In pictures of this story, Theseus and the Minotaur are often shown fighting in the middle of the labyrinth, but there is usually no sign of Ariadne.

People found the idea with the thread so clever that, even today, we talk about following or losing the thread of a conversation, for example.

This is what the labyrinth on Crete may have looked like.

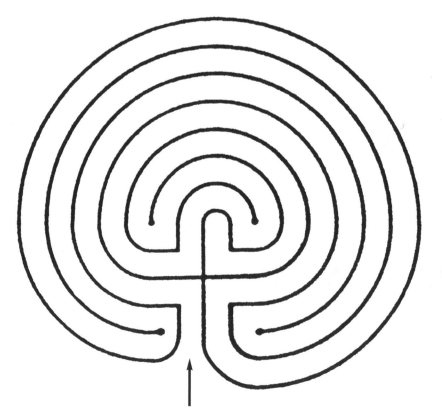

Ariadne's thread will lead you through the
labyrinth to Theseus and the Minotaur.

Where can labyrinths be found?

There are surprisingly few labyrinths that you can actually walk around, but there are many pictures of labyrinths on old stones and coins, and in books and in paintings. Examples of labyrinths can be found in many different countries around the world.

This picture of an Italian with a labyrinth on his tunic was painted about 500 years ago.

These silver coins were found in Greece.

This picture was carved in sandstone by Hopi Indians.

This carving of a labyrinth can be seen in the doorway to a cathedral in Italy.

6

It's amazing how many different shapes and designs there are. This alone shows how popular and important labyrinths must have been, but we still don't know exactly what they were originally used for.

In England people made labyrinths in fields of long grass. They went out into a meadow and cut away the grass to form paths. Some grass labyrinths date from a long time ago and have been so well looked after that they still exist today.

Labyrinths called 'Troja castles' can be found in Sweden. They are made out of large stones with grass paths between them and are always situated near the sea. We know very little about them but perhaps, like in England, people danced from the edge of the labyrinth to the middle and back again!

Two thousand years ago, the Romans liked to have floor mosaics in the shape of labyrinths. Mosaics are made of lots of different small stones put together to form a pattern or a picture.

Mosaics covered the floors of huge rooms. At first glance they look a bit like carpets, as the wonderful patterns were often decorated with plants, animals and other shapes.

Roman labyrinths are mostly square in shape and the path leads you through one quarter of the design before taking you to the next. It is not difficult to imagine the children of rich Roman families walking along the narrow paths of the mosaic labyrinths, or tracing the route with a stick.

There are also modern labyrinths like the one on the right in front of a chapel in Germany. To reach the large flower at the middle follow the dark path that winds its way to the centre.

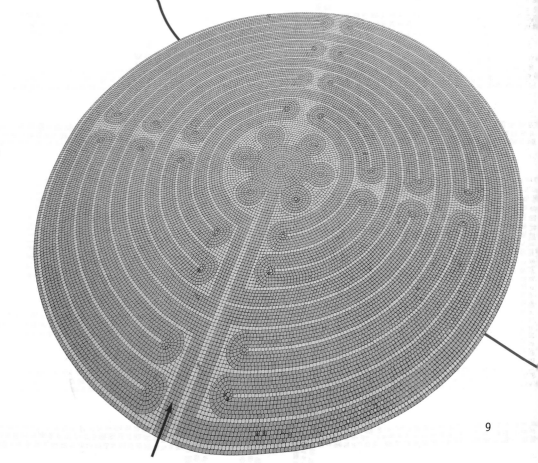

9

Mysterious paths

During the period which art historians call the Gothic Age, the floors of important churches were often decorated with labyrinths. Dating from around 800 years ago, light and dark-coloured stone tiles were laid next to each other to make labyrinths that often covered the whole width of a nave. Perhaps worshippers walked around it while praying or the lines marked the edge of an area used for performing a play like on a stage.

The labyrinth in the floor of Chartres Cathedral in France is particularly big and very well known. If you follow the light-coloured path, you will have to walk nearly 300 metres before reaching the flower-like pattern at the middle! But as an old saying goes, the path you take is more important than actually reaching your goal.

This is what the labyrinth in Chartres Cathedral looks like. Follow the light-coloured path to the middle.

This octagonal labyrinth can be found in the Gothic cathedral of Amiens in France. To reach the middle follow the dark line that starts on the left.

Losing your way!

Pictures of labyrinths can be found in ancient manuscripts and old books written in Greek or Latin. It is in these books that we find the first pictures of mazes, too, in the form of plans made for a big garden. Labyrinths and mazes are not the same and lots of people confuse the two. Even when looking at some of the ancient drawings it is not always clear at first what is what.

Unlike labyrinths, it is very easy to get lost in a maze because there are all sorts of paths that fork off in different directions and then lead nowhere! In a labyrinth, however, you will always reach the middle unless you give up halfway. There is no way you can get confused and all you need is patience and determination.

The earliest known drawing of a maze was made by a doctor from Venice who also invented a secret code which he used when writing explanations of his drawings. Can you find the way to the middle?

This looks very confusing! It is in fact a maze made up of several labyrinths.

Do you think you have to go up and down all the paths to get to the middle?

Games for maze-lovers

Here are some original plans of mazes from old books. Start at the point marked with an arrow and see if you can find the right path to the middle or to the way-out.

**Watch out!
One of these is actually a labyrinth
and not a maze at all.
Which one is it?**

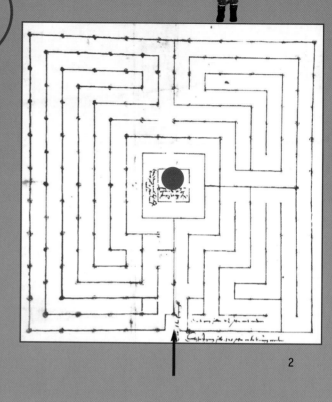

2

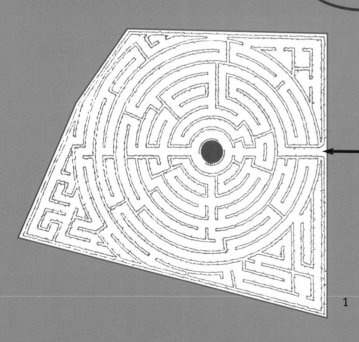

1

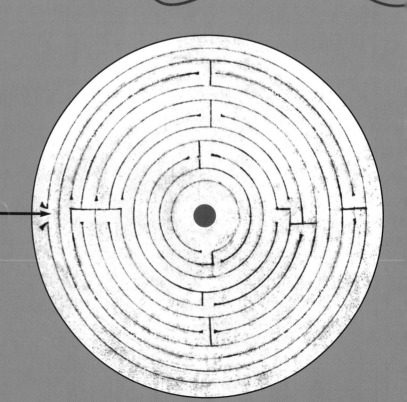

3

14

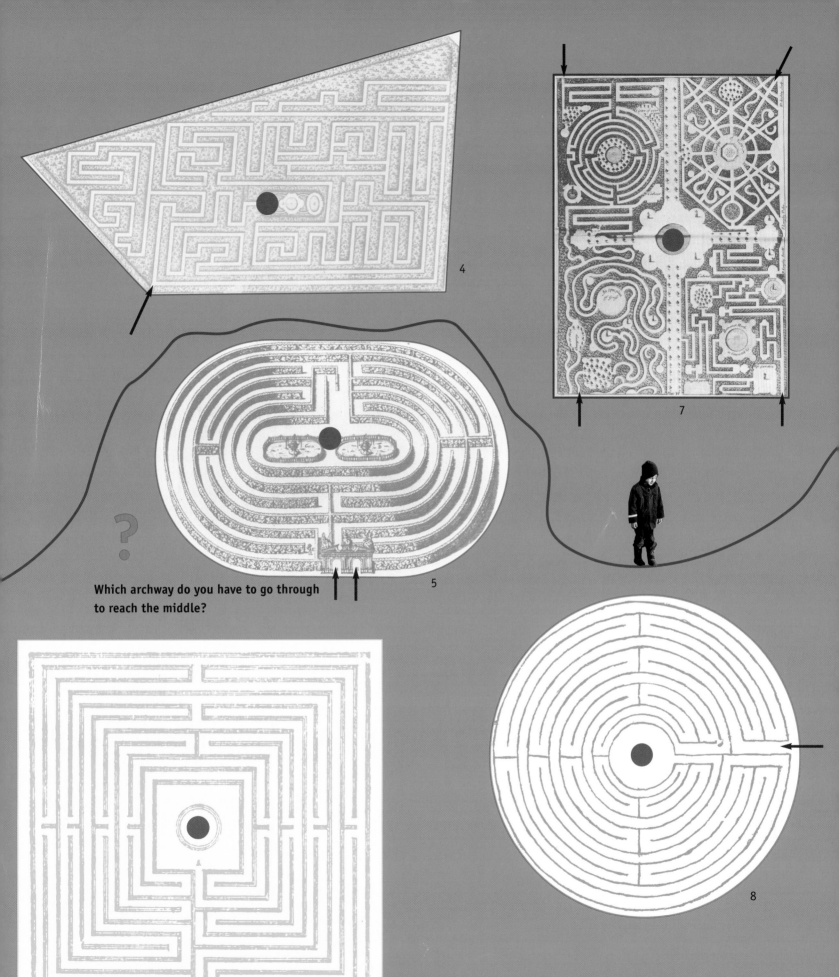

Which archway do you have to go through to reach the middle?

4

7

5

?

6

8

Hide-and-seek between the hedges

There was a time when labyrinths and mazes became very popular, especially during the summer months. People who were rich enough had their own hedge maze planted in their large gardens. It might be easy to find the middle of a labyrinth, but mind-boggling mazes are more fun because you can play catch and hide-and seek between the hedges, too. The owners of the palaces and country houses where the mazes were built also liked to play in them. They shrieked and laughed as they wandered through the maze and fell into each other's arms with relief when they found the way out again!

Gardeners planted hedges in close rows leaving enough room for narrow paths in-between. They had to keep the hedges very well trimmed so that they would become nice and thick. Old hedges that have been well looked after can still be seen today in many castle gardens. The next time you have the chance, go into a maze and try to find the way to the middle.

There are several possibilities for getting to the middle of this maze. But how do you get out again?

Gardens for getting lost in!

One of the most famous hedge mazes in the world is in the park of an ancient royal palace in England. It is at Hampton Court Palace just outside London and is more than 300 years old (below).

Can you find the quickest way to the middle?

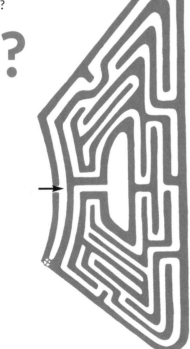

B. Langley *Invent et delin:*   *Plate* IIII   T. Bowles *Sculp*

Some landscape gardeners liked mazes so much that they wanted to fill whole parks with them, as you can see in the drawing above.

The maze on the left is also in England, in the grounds of Longleat House in Wiltshire. The one on the right, however, is in Germany.

Summer in the Palace Gardens

Mazes often have a small tower or a platform in the middle. From above, you can get a good view of the paths and watch other people taking wrong turnings as they try to find their way to the middle.

The paths in the maze shown here in the palace grounds at Schönbrunn in Vienna, Austria, lead to a platform built around a very old tree. From up there you can see the whole maze.

This new labyrinth (below) is like an adventure playground. There are lots of exciting things for children to try out, especially the hopping games. There is a huge metal xylophone where you can play tunes by hopping from one note to the other. Or you can climb the musical pole and ring the bell at the top. There is also a giant kaleidoscope and a mathematical puzzle as well as many other interesting things to investigate.

Here's a tip in case you get lost in a maze: if you always keep the hedge on your right and take every right-hand turn, you will normally find the way out again, even if it means walking a long, long way. The same goes the other way round when trying to find the way to the middle.

Crazy mazes!

About 500 years ago, an Italian designed these labyrinths in the shape of a dog and a crab. Can you find your way to the dog's head and to the middle of the crab?

?

The entrance to this exciting maze in the shape of a ship is at the bottom. Can you find the way to the top of the mast?

Sometimes we use the words 'labyrinth' or 'maze' to describe something difficult or complicated to understand. We feel we are in a labyrinth when we are confused or disorientated, for example when we are wandering through narrow twisting streets in an old town or passing through a hall of mirrors at a fairground. Things are just not as they seem.

Take a look at the spiral on the right. Is this an unusual labyrinth or is it something completely different?

This huge figure is also a labyrinth, but, here, you have to walk along the low walls and not the paths in-between. The artist Daniel Spoerri designed this unusual piece of art for the garden of his house in Tuscany, Italy.

Make your own maze!

Designing a maze or a labyrinth is no easy matter – in fact, it is really quite complicated! If you want to try and draw a labyrinth, why not follow these instructions. (Use a piece of squared paper to make things easier).

To start with, draw a cross and four dots as shown below.

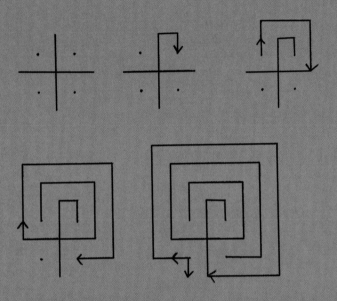

If you want to draw a larger labyrinth, make the cross in the middle bigger. Then follow the same principle ...

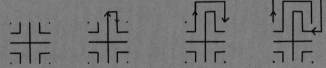

... until it looks like this.

24

Some farmers make mazes in their fields. Why not try to plant your own small version of a maze using cress?

How to make your own maze

- Cover the bottom of a wooden tray with a sheet of plastic.
- Put 2 or 3cm of soil on top.
- Design the path through your maze by placing plastic building blocks on the soil, pressing them down slightly so that they keep their position.

(It is easier to make a maze rather than a labyrinth. Just mark out a path from the edge to the middle and then make the side paths and dead ends).

- Sow cress seeds so that they land between the building blocks and water the cress regularly.
- When the cress has grown 2 or 3 cm high, take the blocks out carefully and then you will be able to see the maze!

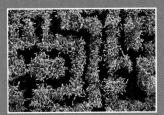

Fun labyrinths

If you've got enough space in a garden or on a beach, you could
make your own labyrinth using pieces of string, stones, sand or
large pebbles. Or you could draw one on a paved area with chalk.
It's great fun running around a labyrinth with your friends, or
chasing each other without treading on the lines. You can use the
drawing on the right to help you.

Answers

Page 3: Yes, you have to go through every bit of the labyrinth before you reach the middle.

Page 12:

Page 13: No, you do not have to go down every path. There are several ways of reaching the middle. For example:

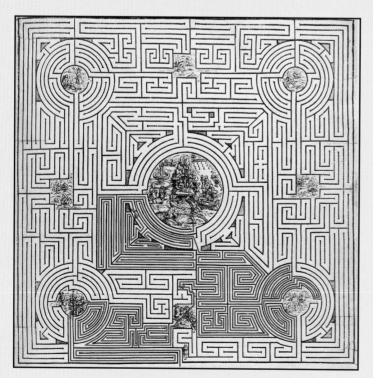

Pages 14/15: number 8 is a labyrinth. The following paths lead to the middle:

1

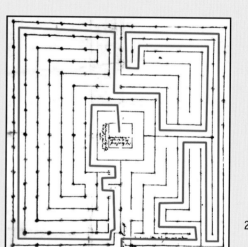

2

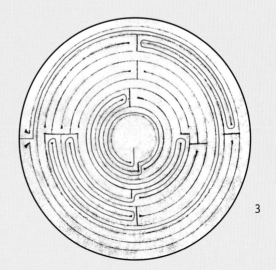

3

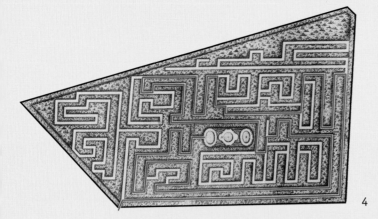

4

Pages 16/17: The way out is via exit A!

Page 19:

5

You have to go through the archway on the left to reach the middle.

Page 22:

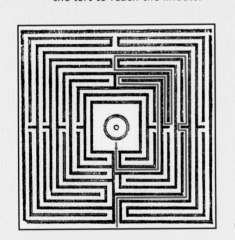

6

Page 23: The spiral at the top of page 23 isn't actually a spiral or a labyrinth at all. If you look carefully, you will see that it is a series of circles. The pattern behind them forms an optical illusion.

7

Labyrinth letters

Don't these letters look strange? They are difficult to read, too, as the sentences go round and round in a spiral and you have to keep turning the paper to read the words.

Why don't you try to write a labyrinth letter yourself? It's fun and perhaps your friends would be surprised to receive a labyrinth letter or a maze message!

These two labyrinth letters were written several hundred years ago in very curly writing. But don't they look lovely even if they are difficult to read?

Labyrinth letter

To: _____   Date: _____

   _____

   _____

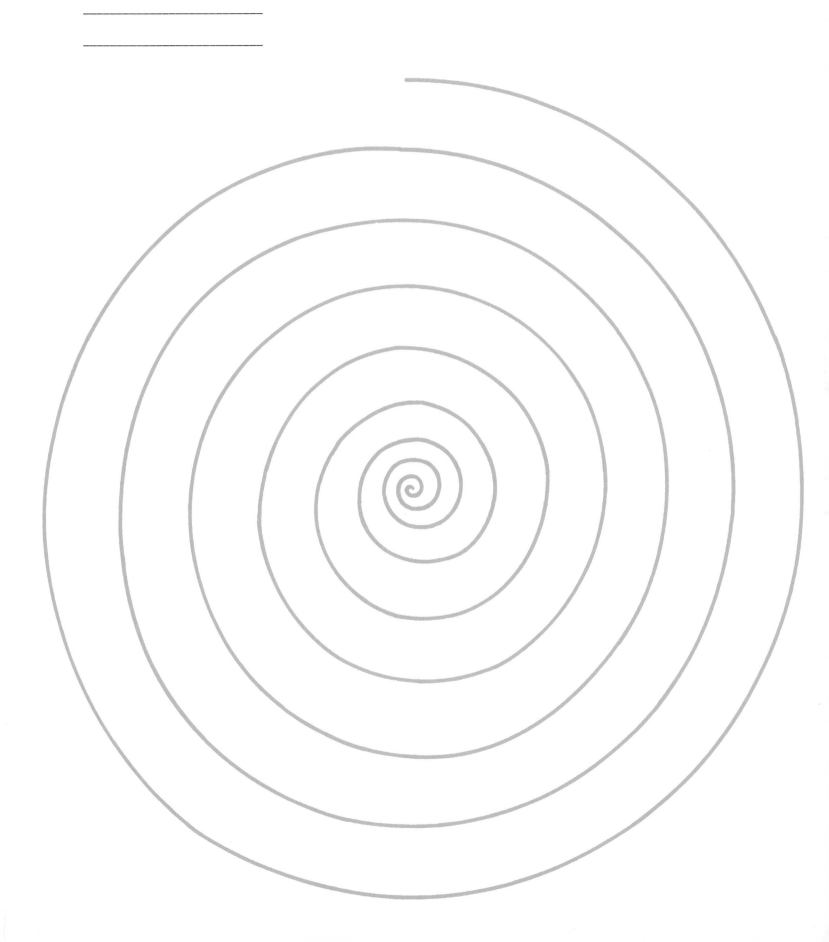

HIC INCLVSVS VITAM PERDIT

To: _____

_____

_____

To: _____   Date: _____

_____

_____